Nature's Fury
LANDSLIDES

John Hamilton

ABDO
& Daughters

VISIT US AT

WWW.ABDOPUB.COM

Published by ABDO Publishing Company, 4940 Viking Drive, Suite 622, Edina, Minnesota 55435.
Copyright ©2006 by Abdo Consulting Group, Inc. International copyrights reserved in all countries.
No part of this book may be reproduced in any form without written permission from the publisher.
ABDO & Daughters™ is a trademark and logo of ABDO Publishing Company.

Printed in the United States.

Editor: Paul Joseph
Graphic Design: John Hamilton
Cover Design: Neil Klinepier
Cover Photo: Corbis
Interior Photos and Illustrations:
   Corbis, p. 8, 9, 10, 11, 12, 13, 14, 15, 16, 17, 18-19, 21, 26, 27, 28, 29
   AP/Wide World Photos, p. 1, 3, 6-7, 20, 22, 23, 24, 26, 32

Library of Congress Cataloging-in-Publication Data

Hamilton, John, 1959–
   Landslides / John Hamilton.
      p. cm. — (Nature's fury)
      Includes index.
   ISBN 1-59679-331-7
   1. Landslides—Juvenile literature. [1. Landslides.] I. Title.

QE599.A2H36 2006
551.3'07—dc22
                                                2005046532

CONTENTS

A boy walks through the remains of his village after mudslides struck parts of Quezon Province, Philippines.

LANDSLIDE!

ON CHRISTMAS DAY, DECEMBER 25, 2003, 24 PEOPLE CELEBRATED the holiday at the Saint Sophia youth camp in California's San Bernardino Mountains, about 60 miles (97 km) east of Los Angeles. The camp was located in Waterman Canyon. More than 3.5 inches (9 cm) of rain fell that day, saturating the ground. In October and November of that year, wildfires had scorched the area, leaving the steep hills without the vegetation that normally holds the ground together. It was a recipe for disaster.

Suddenly, without warning, a section of a hillside gave way. A wall of mud raced downhill and spilled into the stream channel at the bottom of the canyon, engulfing everything in its path. It traveled faster than people could run, leaving them helpless in a sea of muddy water, branches, logs, boulders, rocks, and other debris. Even less than a foot of this destructive mix was enough to knock people down.

Twisted playground equipment at the Saint Sophia youth camp.

As the mudslide continued its rampage through the canyon, it buried houses and cabins and anything else unlucky enough to be swept up in its path. By the time rescue crews arrived at the camp, they found two dead bodies partially buried in the thick, gray-colored muck. In some places, the mud was 12 to 15 feet (3.7 to 4.6m) thick.

Rescue workers faced very slippery conditions. They sometimes fell into mud up to their hips. One rescued man had been stuck in waist-deep mud. His feet were trapped by a log. His rescuers cut the log free and then carried him to safety.

A third dead body was found at a nearby trailer park. Thirteen other

Rescue crews remove debris by hand as they search for bodies at a washed out bridge over Waterman Creek near San Bernardino, California, December 29, 2003.

people, mostly children from the youth camp, were missing. Authorities presumed they were swept away and buried by the killer landslide. In addition, dozens of people were injured, and many roads and bridges were washed out from the flooding.

Landslides are geological hazards. They are common almost everywhere in the United States. The U.S. government estimates that between 25 and 50 people are killed each year because of landslides. Nearly $2 billion in damage is done in the U.S. by this relentless force of nature. Around the world, landslides kill thousands of people each year, and cause many billions of dollars in damage.

Landslides usually strike without warning. They happen most often during heavy rains, earthquakes, or volcanic eruptions. It is hard to predict where a landslide will strike next. The steepest terrain, where most landslides occur, is often in unpopulated wilderness areas. But sometimes the ground collapses in places where many people live. The worst landslide in recorded history happened on December 16, 1920, in Kansu, China. A major earthquake there caused a deadly series of landslides, killing more than 180,000 people.

An 81-year-old woman sits crying as residents sift through the remains of buildings after a mudslide tore through Shangfang Village in China's Zhejiang province in August, 2002. The mudslide killed 21 people.

THE SCIENCE OF LANDSLIDES

A LANDSLIDE IS THE SUDDEN COLLAPSE OF A LARGE SECTION OF a hillside. Landslides usually strike on steep slopes. Mountainous areas that are made of rocks, which produce sandy soils, are very prone to landslides.

People who witness landslides often report a roaring and rumbling noise, followed by a wall of rocks, mud, trees, and boulders moving rapidly downhill, often in the streambeds of narrow canyons. A fast-moving landslide engulfs and destroys almost everything in its path. Behind it, the earth is stripped to the bedrock.

Landslides happen all over the world. In the United States, they most often strike in the Rocky Mountains, the Appalachian Mountains, and in the states that make up the Pacific Coastal Range, which include California, Oregon, and Washington. Landslides are also common in parts of Alaska and Hawaii.

Debris flow is a technical term used by scientists. It describes the rapid downhill motion of rocks, soil, water, and vegetation. Depending on how much water is present, debris flows can be either landslides or mudslides. Landslides are drier kinds

A home lies in ruins after a landslide in Seattle, Washington.

A landslide wiped out this neighborhood in
Las Colinas, El Salvador, in January, 2001.

A section of California's Highway One was washed out by a landslide in 1982.

Deadly mudslides on December 23, 2003, killed more than 200 people in Leyte Province, central Philippines.

of debris flows. Mudslides are wet, shallow, fast-moving debris flows. A slump is what happens when a whole section of earth moves in one piece. It leaves behind a smooth rock face. Scientists also call this kind of landslide a rotational block slip.

Landslides move downhill at different speeds. Some move only a few inches each year. These are called "creep" landslides. The fastest are mudslides. They usually flow about 10 miles per hour (16 km/hr), but sometimes they move several times faster.

What exactly causes a landslide? The ground we see is made of several layers of topsoil, which rests on top of hard bedrock. Bedrock is made of gravel, rocks, boulders, or huge slabs of solid rock. When intense storms dump several inches of rain on an area, the water percolates through the layers of topsoil. When enough rain seeps into the ground, the soil is saturated—it becomes a slippery, soupy layer of mud. Sometimes the weight of the water-saturated soil itself is enough to cause it to slide downhill. Other times landslides and mudslides are triggered by other events, like earthquakes or volcanoes. As the landslide travels downhill, it picks up debris like rocks, trees, and vegetation. This makes the landslide even more destructive.

Several things work together to determine when landslides occur, and how severe they will be. Most important is the role of water. Soil usually clings to the bedrock, the underlying hillside, because of gravitational pull and friction. But when intense rainstorms occur, the water lubricates the layers. The soil is saturated, which loosens it. The looser the soil, the better chance that it will slide downhill.

Water is very heavy. Combined with gravity, it is a very powerful force in creating landslides and mudslides. A two-inch (5-cm) rainfall over a 24-hour period adds about 10 pounds (4.5 kg) of water to each square foot of soil. On a piece of ground the size of a typical backyard, that adds an extra 50,000 pounds (22,680 kg) of weight to the soil.

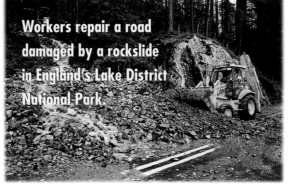
Workers repair a road damaged by a rockslide in England's Lake District National Park.

Water naturally wants to flow downhill, and in many cases it takes the soil with it in the form of a landslide or mudslide. The steeper the slope of the hill, the more likely a landslide will happen. The most destructive landslides happen on very steep slopes. Gentle slopes can have landslides, too, but these take many years to move downhill. You can sometimes spot these "creeps" by observing fenceposts or telephone poles tilted in one direction.

The kind of soil on a hillside is also important. Looser soils are more likely to cause landslides because there is little to keep them intact. Bedrock made of sandstone, granites, and mica create porous soils that move easily. Sticky soils with high clay content are less likely to have landslides. The clay content absorbs water slowly and makes the soil stick together.

Thick vegetation plays an important role in keeping the ground intact. Roots tend to hold soil together. Most trees have deep roots and are very good at

Landslides caused this home to crash down a hillside in Laguna Beach, California, in June, 2005. At least 18 homes were destroyed.

strengthening the soil. Areas that have recently been burned by wildfires, or had trees cut down by loggers, are in danger of landslides. The roots of dead plants quickly decay or turn brittle, losing their ability to keep soil from sliding downhill.

Knowing how land was used in the past is a good way to predict landslides. Human activity often increases the chances of landslides. Danger signs include heavy deforestation, cutting roads through hillsides, and piling heavy material, such as mine tailings or dirt from construction projects, onto slopes. As cities grow outward into steep wilderness areas, much land is cleared of vegetation to make room for houses. This weakens the soil, making landslides and mudslides more likely.

LAHARS

VOLCANOES CAN KILL IN MANY DIFFERENT WAYS. THE BLAST from an eruption can easily kill thousands, but the aftereffects can be even more lethal. For example, the 1883 eruption of Krakatau in the Sunda Strait, a narrow stretch of water between Java and Sumatra, caused a tsunami that killed nearly 40,000 people. The blast itself caused no known deaths.

Deadly volcano aftereffects can include lava flows, superheated airflows, tsunamis, and poisonous gasses. One of the most deadly killers, however, is mud. A *lahar* is a mudflow created when soil and rock mixed with water rush down the sides of a volcano. The name is a term used in Indonesia, where mudflows from volcanoes are common hazards. But how do you get mud from a volcano?

Many volcanoes are high mountains with deep snow packs blanketing the summits. When eruptions occur, hot ash and gasses sometimes flow across the snow packs. The ice and snow melt rapidly, creating a debris-filled mudslide. The lahar then sweeps down the mountain, destroying everything in its path, sometimes traveling many miles from the base of the volcano.

Some lahars gain an incredible amount of volume and speed as they rush downhill. These unstoppable disasters have been measured as large as 132 feet (40 m) thick, with speeds up to 30 miles per hour (48 km/hr).

Washington's Mount St. Helens erupted on May 18, 1980, with the

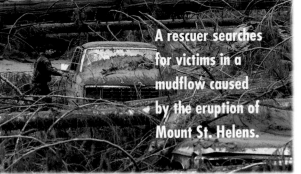

A rescuer searches for victims in a mudflow caused by the eruption of Mount St. Helens.

An aerial photo, with Mount St. Helens still smoldering in the background, showing the devastation of the eruption's mudflows.

explosive force of a 10-megaton bomb. It created one of the largest landslides ever witnessed. The entire north slope of the mountain exploded outward. Making matters worse, tons of melted ice and snow from the volcano's summit mixed with ash, mud, and debris and rushed into several river valleys. The mudflows created massive destruction.

Many people who lived far from the volcano thought they were safe. But they were surprised when the mudflows roared downriver, swallowing up houses and businesses and claiming many lives. Some of the mudflows were more than 1,800 feet (549 m) wide. The mud was so choked with debris and ash that it was as thick as wet cement.

Columbian government, ignored the warnings. They thought the scientists were raising the alarm needlessly. The town of Armero was nearly 45 miles (72 km) from the base of the volcano. Surely, they were safe. After all, the volcano hadn't erupted in 140 years. Tragically, they turned out to be very wrong.

On the night of November 13, the ground began to shake. Pottery jars shattered on dirt floors. The roof tiles of many adobe homes loosened and fell to the ground. Some people were alarmed, but most went back to bed. "It's only Nevado del Ruiz," they thought.

Usually at night the townspeople could see an orange glow from the distant volcano. On this night, the view was obscured by a storm blowing across the summit. People had no idea a major eruption was taking place. Ice and snow from the summit of the volcano rapidly melted from the hot clouds of gas and ash. The mudflow quickly swept down the canyons on the side of the mountain. It was an unstoppable wall of mud and rock, burying everything in its path.

It took the lahar only two and a half hours to reach Armero. Most people were asleep. As the mudflow approached, some people heard a strange

The town of Armero, Columbia, was destroyed when volcanic debris flows called lahars swept down from the erupting Nevado del Ruiz volcano.

Two muddy survivors walk away from the destruction of Armero.

swishing and rumbling noise. If anyone had looked out their window that night into the gloom, they would have been horrified to see a rushing wall of tree-filled black mud. Within minutes, the lahar had swallowed up the entire town.

Some people made it safely to higher ground, but most of the townsfolk were crushed to death, or drowned in the sea of mud. The next day, rescue crews came to Armero, but only a few victims could be dug out of the muck. Twenty three thousand people, three fourths of the town, perished that awful night. Several other villages in the area were also swept away or buried by the lahar.

It is small comfort to the victims of Armero, but some good did come from the eruption of Nevado del Ruiz. People have a greater respect for the peril faced by communities in the path of lahars. Scientists and governments are creating new ways to warn communities that are in danger. The U.S. Geological Survey now has teams of geologists with portable volcano observatories that can quickly be sent anywhere in the world where a volcano awakes. Hopefully, with a better understanding of local history, accurate hazard mapping, and advanced warning systems, future death and destruction can be kept to a minimum.

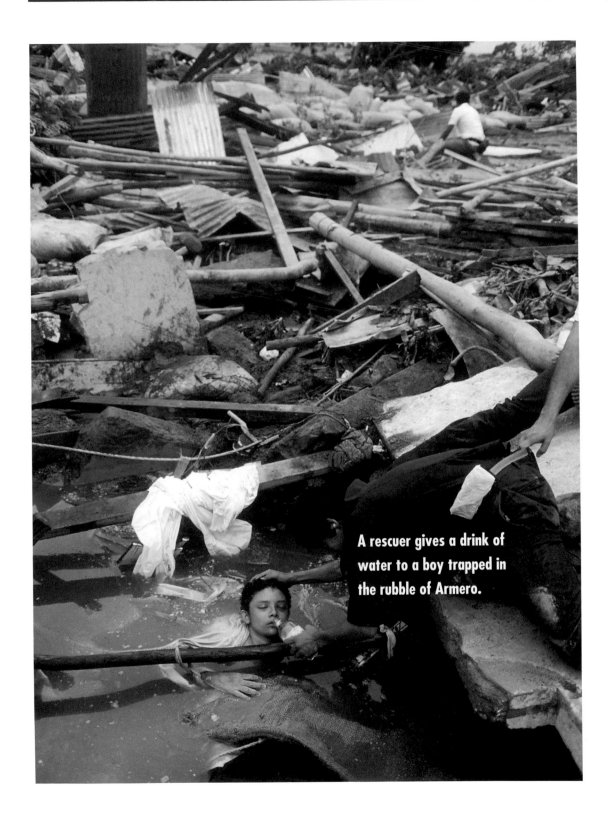

A rescuer gives a drink of water to a boy trapped in the rubble of Armero.

THE LA CONCHITA LANDSLIDES

IN JANUARY 2005, POWERFUL STORMS BATTERED THE CALIFORNIA coastline. For many days, record amounts of rain fell on already saturated hillsides. For areas already prone to mudslides, the potential for disaster was very high.

The small coastal town of La Conchita sits just southeast of the city of Santa Barbara. It is built on a narrow strip of land, nestled between the Pacific Ocean and steep bluffs. The hills have a history of being unstable. In 1995, a massive mudslide buried many houses, but took no lives. However, on January 10, 2005, tragedy finally struck.

A woman uses a dog to search for La Conchita landslide victims.

More than four inches (10 cm) of rain fell the night before. When residents woke up, they found the main highway blocked by muddy runoff from the hills. People began cleaning the streets of mud, taking photos, and talking with neighbors. They didn't realize that behind them lurked a killer, a towering bluff that was supersaturated with rain.

An aerial view of the mudslide that killed 10 people in La Conchita, California, on January 10, 2005.

California Governor Arnold Schwarzenegger views the devastation of La Conchita from a helicopter.

At about 12:30 p.m., the hillside collapsed. People heard a roaring noise that echoed through the town. Looking up, they saw a whole section of the slope turn to liquid. The mudslide then rushed into the town like a terrible, debris-filled brown river, burying houses and anything else in its path. The entire event lasted less than 30 seconds, but in that short time 10 people were killed, buried in the fast-moving mudflow. Fourteen others were injured. The mudslide also destroyed or seriously damaged 36 houses. Cars and trucks were swept away and crushed like toys.

Stunned survivors emerged from the mud, clutching possessions or pets in their hands. Many people frantically tried to find loved ones. One man lost his wife and three daughters. Rescue crews and firefighters soon arrived. Armed with shovels, listening devices, and rescue dogs, they worked tirelessly all that day and through the night, searching for anyone who might be alive and trapped in the debris. As time passed, and hours turned to days, it became clear that there were no more survivors. The mudslide had taken its grim toll.

A street in La Conchita is flooded with mud and debris following the landslide.

W SURFSIDE ST

Governor Arnold Schwarzenegger later visited the devastated town and declared a state emergency at the site. The governor tried to lift the spirits of rescue workers and townspeople. "We have seen the power of nature cause damage and despair," he said, "but we will match that power with our own resolve."

Although some residents wanted to move away from the dangerous area, most have vowed to remain in the free-spirited community. Many said they were not afraid, and want to continue living in the beautiful coastal town. Said Governor Schwarzenegger, "I am going to help them so they can come back here. We will do everything that we can to make it a safe area."

Despite the governor's best intentions, and the desire of the townspeople, it seems very likely that more mudslides will plague the town of La Conchita. Geologists warn that hazards still lurk above the town. At this moment in time, science lacks the understanding to accurately predict exactly when and where the next mudslide will strike. Landslide experts agree that it is only a matter of time.

PROTECT YOURSELF

DOZENS OF PEOPLE ARE KILLED EACH YEAR FROM LANDSLIDES in the United States. There are some things you can do to protect yourself from a landslide or mudslide. The most important thing is prevention. Many landslides happen during bad weather. Most lives are lost in stormy weather at night. In conditions like these, it is too late. Know your risks beforehand.

In some areas the chances of experiencing a landslide are magnified. These include:

• Places where wildfires or human activity has recently destroyed vegetation. Plant roots help keep the soil in place. When the ground is bare, it is much easier for landslides to occur.

• Areas where landslides have happened before. This is a sure sign that the area you are in is prone to slides. Local experts, including county geologists, county planning departments, or university departments of geology, can alert you if your area has been hit in the past by a landslide.

A 1989 earthquake caused this landslide along California's coastal highway.

• Steep hills and slopes, especially at the bottom of canyon areas.

• Stream or riverbed channels.

• Places where the slope of the ground has recently been changed because of building or road construction.

In addition to finding out if the area you are in is vulnerable to a landslide, you should develop emergency and evacuation plans for your family.

A landslide caused this house to slide off its foundation in Nagaoka, Japan.

A communication plan is very important in case family members are separated. Try to agree on a safe place where you all can meet or check in, similar to the communication plan families create in case of a house fire.

Of course, the best prevention is to move away if you discover you are in an area that is prone to landslides. But if you find yourself in such an area during an intense storm with heavy rainfall, it is important that you listen to the radio or watch television news reports about landslides in your area.

If you spot a sudden increase (and sometimes a decrease) in the water level of a nearby stream or creek, this could be a sign of a debris flow upstream. Be on the lookout for tilted trees or telephone poles. Fences and walls might also start tilting downhill. New holes or bare spots on hillsides are another warning sign. People often hear a low rumbling noise before a debris flow hits.

If you know a landslide or mudslide is about to strike, your best chance of survival is to move quickly away from the path of destruction. Run to the nearest high ground away from the landslide. If you cannot get out of the way, get to a shelter and take cover under a heavy piece of furniture, like a desk or table.

After the landslide has passed, stay away from the area. More flooding or debris flows might happen on the same site. Check for injured or trapped people in the debris, but only if you can do so safely without entering the flow zone. Call 911 for help, and report any broken gas or electrical utilities. Each year many people are injured or killed after landslides because of broken utilities or roadways.

After a landslide, special engineers called geotechnical experts can tell your family how to reduce landslide problems and risks in the future.

A landslide destroyed this home in Laguna Beach, California, in June, 2005.

A man tries to clean up a street after a 2002 mudslide in the village of Orosi, Costa Rica. Five people were reported missing and 20 houses destroyed by the mudslide.

GLOSSARY

BEDROCK

The hard layer of earth that lies beneath topsoil. Bedrock can be made of gravel, rocks, boulders, or large slabs of solid rock. After a severe landslide, all that is left behind is often bare bedrock.

CREEP

A creep is a type of landslide that moves very slowly, sometimes only a few inches each year.

DEBRIS FLOW

The rapid downhill motion of rocks, soil, water, and vegetation in a landslide. Debris flow is a term often used by scientists. It describes both dry rockslides and wet mudslides.

GEOLOGICAL SURVEY

The United States Geological Survey was created in 1879. It is an independent science agency that is part of the Department of the Interior. It researches and collects facts about the land of the United States, and the world, giving us a better understanding of our natural resources.

GEOLOGIST

A scientist who is an expert on the physical nature and history of the earth. Geologists learn about landslides by studying different rock types, the composition of soil layers, and how water and gravity affect topsoils.

ROTATIONAL BLOCK SLIP

A kind of landslide that occurs when an entire section of a hillside moves downhill in one piece, leaving behind a smooth rock face. Rotational block slips are also called slumps.

SLOPE

The angle at which ground is tilted. Landslides are more likely to occur on slopes that are very steep.

TOPSOIL

Layers of earth that lie atop a hard layer of bedrock. Topsoils that are porous and loose are prone to landslides. Sticky soils with high clay content don't have as many landslides, since the clay absorbs water slowly, which makes the soil stick together.

WILDFIRE

Fires that burn in wilderness areas, like forests or grasslands. Hillsides that have suffered recent wildfires are often prone to landslides after a heavy rain, since the vegetation that normally helps hold the soil together has been burned away.

WEB SITES

WWW.ABDOPUB.COM

Would you like to learn more about landslides? Please visit www.abdopub.com to find up-to-date Web site links about landslides and other natural disasters. These links are routinely monitored and updated to provide the most current information available.

INDEX

Bystanders look over a road damaged after a March 2005 landslide in Aptos, California.